ACE REID AND THE COWPOKES CARTOONS

Ace Reid and the Cowpokes Cartoons

INTRODUCTION BY ELMER KELTON
FOREWORD BY PAT OLIPHANT

UNIVERSITY OF TEXAS PRESS

AUSTIN

Third paperback printing, 2005

Requests for permission to reproduce material from this work should be sent to
Permissions, University of Texas Press, Box 7819, Austin, TX 78713-7819.
www.utexas.edu/utpress/about/bpermission.html

∞ The paper used in this publication meets the minimum requirements of
American National Standard for Information Sciences—Permanence of Paper
for Printed Library Materials, ANSI Z39.48-1984.

LIBRARY OF CONGRESS CATALOGING-IN-PUBLICATION DATA

Reid, Asa E., 1925–
Ace Reid and the cowpokes cartoons / introduction by Elmer Kelton ;
foreword by Pat Oliphant – 1st ed.
    p.   cm – (Southwestern Writers Collection series)

1. Ranch life — Caricatures and cartoons. 2. American wit and humor,
Pictorial. I. Title. II. Series.
NC1429.R434 A4 1999
741.5´973–ddc21   ISBN: 978-0-292-77097-3   98-25330

THIS COLLECTION of cartoons is the most meaningful to me of all collections of Ace's works. At last Cowpokes readers, future cartoonists, and a wider public will be able to see the detailed pen and ink work in each drawing. Without this book, only those few people who have seen the original drawings would ever know of Ace Reid's talent as a pen and ink artist because so much of the fine detail of his work is lost in reproduction for newspaper syndication.

For this realization of my longtime dream—to show Ace, the artist behind the cartoonist—I am most grateful to Richard Holland and the Southwestern Writers Collection, who made my dream of this publication come true.

To the steadfast readers, editors, and publishers of Cowpokes cartoons whose loyalty has kept Cowpokes alive for fifty years, I wish to dedicate this book with love, appreciation, and thanks.

—Madge Reid

SOUTHWESTERN WRITERS COLLECTION SERIES

*The Southwestern Writers Collection Series
originates from the Southwestern Writers Collection,
an archive and literary center
established at Southwest Texas State University
to celebrate the region's writers and literary heritage.*

CONTENTS

Foreword by Pat Oliphant *9*

Introduction: Ace Reid by Elmer Kelton *11*

Work *23*

Economics *59*

Bankers *75*

Weather *93*

Ma *109*

Outsiders *141*

Friends & Neighbors *159*

Ace at the drawing board in his studio at the Draggin' S Ranch

FOREWORD

by Pat Oliphant

I GREW UP IN SOUTH AUSTRALIA, a state of Australia covering some two and a half times the area of Texas. There are seven states in Australia, or rather, six states and a territory, some smaller and some bigger, and South Australia, while not a pissant, is only a middling-sized state. I mention all this for several reasons, the leading one being to demonstrate that when it comes to size, Australians are as much given to bovine by-product boasting as any Texan. This is one possible reason why, at least in my personal experience, Texans and Australians get along so well. Secondly, South Australia is covered for the most part by sand, rocks, scorpions, and snakes, which makes it a first cousin to the moon and Texas . . . and I have been to Texas. I have no idea why, but for some reason, such places tend to produce more than their share of people with a creative bent. For this I have no theory other than the obvious one—that in these places, given the focusing qualities of isolation, a person is inclined to develop a more active and acute imagination. Or, rather, the innate imagination is sharpened and sensitized. It also develops a sense of humor.

Speaking of cartooning—and we weren't, but how else can I segue into this—Australia has a great tradition of cartooning art which has been nurtured by these circumstances since early times. A cartoon is, after all, an evocation and exaggeration of the recognizable. Conjure up a set of experiences, place them all in a recognizable setting, give it all a stretch and a twist, and you have the ingredients of a successful cartoon. One successful Australian artist, Eric Jolliffe, who was, of all things, English by birth, became so shaped and sculpted by his wanderings and working on the remote, hard-scrabble farms and cattle stations of the Outback that when he began putting down his humorous observations of the vast Back of Beyond in graphic form he was immediately embraced by his reading public, and rightly so, as a great cartoonist. He was still working when I first met him ten years ago, and he regaled me then with the full method and procedure for parting a bull calf from his testicles by the venerable biting method. I never saw that depicted in his cartoons, but he took a wicked relish in telling it to someone he recognized as likely to pale at the thought. But Jolliffe was a man totally immersed in his work, and in his search for the authentic he rendered drawings accurate down to the last random bend of a piece of fencing wire. These were backgrounds and details honed to perfection by decades of simply looking. Looking, and employing that other great artists' and writers' tool . . . remembering.

And when I looked at the work of Ace Reid, I thought of Eric Jolliffe.

Ace Reid! My god, most cartoonists would kill for a name like that. In fact, when I found it was no longer occupied, I was sorely tempted to adopt it as my own, and would have had I not been so far down the road. I then formulated Oliphant's First Law of Cartooning, it being that all young, aspiring cartoonists should change their names early.

In cartooning, the sublime and the ridiculous are never separated by much. In Ace's work (I call him Ace, he doesn't call me much of anything), as with Jolliffe's, the sublime is in the details. The truck looks like a soreback, thirty-eight-year-old truck should look, with every dent, every rust streak, gouge, and broken mirror in its proper place. The cattle are goofy the way all cattle are goofy. So are the horses, though some of them, as in life, are smarter than the human folks. Look at the homesteads, the lean-to structures, the posts, the fences, the bobwar (called, in Australia, barbed wire), the hay bales, the mail boxes, the rutted trails, the washouts, the arroyos . . . it's all there. He could have been, in many cases, drawing the Outback. The people are laconic, a source of humor in itself. And also long suffering. And relentlessly recognizable. Ace, you can see, realized that the key to every cartoon situation is recognition, that cartooning is simply a conspiracy between the cartoonist and the reader and recognition is the element which warms the relationship. The exaggeration and the caption are bonuses. The combination is magic.

Ace's work has a magic of its own, however, and it owes nothing to anyone else. He was a man of his time, and he recorded it through the lens of his own gentle sense of hilarity. It's a grin and a nod type of humor. And that type is, for what he was trying to say, no doubt the best kind. It's my sense that Ace was a kindly soul whom I would have liked to sit and tell lies with. I bet he wouldn't have told me about chomping on some lil' ol' bull calf.

But who knows . . . ?

Washington, D.C.
March 1998

INTRODUCTION: ACE REID

by Elmer Kelton

WHEN I CAME TO KNOW ACE REID, he had developed his first regular outlet for his Cowpokes cartoons in Stanley Frank's then-new *West Texas Livestock Weekly,* published in San Angelo, Texas. We had in common that both of us had grown up on West Texas ranches. Like me, he was a young veteran of World War II, and our careers were in their beginning stages. He used to grin and say we were both barefoot at the time. Actually, he said *barefooted.*

I was writing agricultural news for the daily *San Angelo Standard-Times* when Ace decided he should begin syndicating his cartoons to more newspapers. He was unable to find a national syndicator who saw a future in his work, so he decided to do it for himself. He approached Houston Harte, publisher of the *Standard,* with a poor-boy proposition that appealed to Mr. Harte's sentiments. Ace would offer him free use of the cartoons if the paper would furnish him however many mats he needed to send to other publications. Mr. Harte, who always had a soft spot for people with ambition and focus, agreed.

The only problem was that they did not clear the deal with Bill Woody, the business manager. For years Woody kept sending Ace a monthly bill, and the bills got larger and larger as Ace's syndication list grew. Every so often Ace would have to drive from Kerrville to San Angelo and get Mr. Harte to intercede.

Ace was a jovial "good old boy" who could get along with almost anybody, but for whatever reason, he and Bill Woody could never seem to go around the same side of the telephone pole together.

BORN IN 1925 at Lelia Lake in the Texas Panhandle, Ace Reid was a child of the 1930s depression, which hit farm and ranch people as hard as anyone—sometimes harder, because many were uprooted from the land to which they had been born and set adrift in a world they did not fully know or understand. Even those who managed to survive labored under the shadow of the sheriff's hammer. The Reid family, like the others, worked hard and lived Spartan lives. Before they spent a nickel, they squeezed it until the buffalo bawled.

Though Ace's cartooning career started after the depression was over, the harsh memories colored his work. The people whose lives he reflected in his drawings had not forgotten what hardship and heartache they endured, and they never forgot that a drought or a bad break in the livestock market could easily push them back under that dark cloud.

Humor has always been a hallmark of ranch folk in general. It has given them strength to endure whatever slings and arrows outrageous fortune might hurl at them. Indeed, some have said that had they not been able to laugh at their troubles, or at least smile, they might have been driven crazy. This is reflected in many of Ace's cartoons, for beneath their surface humor often lies a strong sense of irony, a quiet desperation. Humor is all that stands between the characters and despair.

Some years ago the lamb market took a sudden and precipitous drop, and a small group of lamb feeders lost half a million dollars before they had time to take full stock of what was happening. One told me, "The buzzards have quit my lamb-feeding pens. They've taken to roosting at my house."

He had a choice between laughing and crying, and he chose to laugh. It was a strained laugh, to be sure, but it was better than despair. He survived.

Those were Ace Reid's kind of people. The hard economic realities of ranch life are reflected in his work. They are there when Jake watches the truck hauling away the thirty-two-cent calves he was holding for thirty-six and finally sold for twenty-eight. They are there in the lean ribs of his prickly-pear-eating cows and in the boxy little ranch houses bereft of conveniences more modern than the rub board, the kerosene lamp, and the one-holer out back. They are there in the many confrontations between the rancher and his banker.

Ace knew the rancher's problems firsthand, having learned them by following his rancher-trader father, Ace Sr., to the livestock auction barns and trading pens in the region around his home town of Electra, west of Wichita Falls. Ace claimed that school never taught him as much as he learned sitting in the high seats at one auction or another, waiting to help Old Man Ace load out whatever cattle or horses he might buy at the day's sale. There he listened to ranchers' and cowboys' stories and absorbed the lore of the land. There he watched the daily testing of other people's dreams and, all too often, saw them dashed by the vagaries of an unpredictable market.

There, too, he studied the lessons in salesmanship that would gradually make his name and his work famous throughout the West and Southwest. From his father he learned that it took salesmanship to convince a potential buyer that a set of droughted-out cows lank in the flanks and short on teeth were just what he needed. Ace Sr. knew that to sell a product he first had to sell himself. He could sell bagged ice to an Eskimo, and Ace Jr. gradually acquired the trait.

People who first came to know him in his later years had a hard time believing that Ace Jr. as a young man was shy by nature, that he had to push to make himself get out and mix with the public. He made a conscious effort to become outgoing and assertive. He succeeded, probably even beyond his dreams. The mature Ace was anything but shy. When he walked into a room, everyone knew that Ace Reid had arrived. Gregarious, always ready to joke and spin yarns or pull some kind of prank, he no longer had to work at living up to the image. He became the image.

It took him a while to find his true niche in life. He liked cowboys and respected their way of life, but it pleased him best when other people lived it. He determined early on through hard personal experience that the cowboy life was most pleasant taken in small doses. It was too hot or too cold, too dusty or too muddy most of the time, and the pay was poor. It was not the way he intended to spend the rest of his days.

Coming home from the Navy, he nevertheless invested in cattle and wheat as well as an oil drilling outfit. The pickings proved to be slim. Winding up all but broke, he found some success as a salesman, but his primary ambition remained as it had been for years: to become a professional artist. He wanted to chronicle the ranching way of life through his drawings.

Asked once how he came to be a cartoonist, he said it was his only viable alternative to cowboying. "The oil wells went dry, the greenbugs got my wheat, and the bottom fell out of the cow market."

He found an occasional outlet in a horsemen's magazine published by Ed Bateman, but his real break came when he met Stanley Frank, who had just begun publishing a weekly livestock newspaper. Frank had a knack of spotting and encouraging new talent and over time would give several writers their first real start. He and Ace began what would become a lifelong friendship. Through the years, despite the success of his syndication program—at one time he was published in more than four hundred newspapers—Ace always gave *Livestock Weekly* first use of his cartoons. He and Frank worked on trust. In an association that lasted more than forty years, they never wrote up a contract.

In the beginning, the cartoons tended to be mostly one-liner gags. But Ace's craftsmanship as an artist matured rapidly, and so did his subject matter. Many of his cartoons became philosophical, but never heavy-handed. In many respects they resembled the wise *Out Our Way* cartoons drawn in an earlier time by J. R. Williams, whose work Ace always admired.

As Williams had depicted Western life in the 1920s to the 1940s, Ace depicted it as he saw it from the late 1940s on. At its best, it was a dead-on representation of his own life and times.

Occasionally he would draw a cartoon so politically incorrect that it would never pass muster for syndication. Stanley Frank did not back away; he ran them all . . . even one showing a group of nervous neighbors at a Lyndon B. Johnson Ranch barbecue, worrying over the possibility that they might be eating their own beef. Or another, in the 1960s, depicting two cowboys looking lost among a large gathering of minorities at the Poor People's March in Washington, wondering why they did not see more ranchers there.

Ace was forever grateful. He and Madge named their son Stan after Stanley Frank.

Ace in his youth was a working hand on his father's ranch and on other ranches where he hired out. He understood the mentality of the cowboy just as he understood the ways of the ranch owner. He was keenly aware that real cowboy life had little of the romance and glamour portrayed in films and much of popular fiction. He often played on the contrast between reality and public perception, as when Eastern tourists come upon a couple of ragged, dirty, sweaty ranchhands digging postholes and ask, "Could you fellows tell us where we might see real cowboys?"

Ace's cowboys never bested the villain with fists or guns, never dressed in the latest of Western fashions, never had the beautiful show horse with flaxen mane and tail. His cowboys were everlastingly being thrown, stomped, tromped, and dragged through the dirt, mud, rocks, and cactus by rough-haired, rawboned, jug-headed broncs. They were plunging headlong through thorny thickets in pursuit of fleet-footed, wild-eyed outlaw cattle or were being chased to the fence by sharp-horned cows bent on homicide.

They never won the fair schoolmarm and whisked her off into the golden sunset, either. The poor Ma of his cartoons is a plain-looking, underappreciated, overworked little woman who wears a single pathetic flower in her hat and makes her own dresses out of printed feed-sack material. Even so, she is a pearl of great price, though her cowboy husband seldom seems to realize it, or at least to acknowledge it. Jake's idea of sensitivity is to buy Ma a new ax for Christmas. Ace knew cowboy reticence well, for he had worked to overcome it in his early years. Cowboys might brag on their horses until a listener's ears hurt, but to draw from them expressions of affection or appreciation for wives or girlfriends would often be like trying to squeeze milk from a stone.

For that matter, most of Ace's male characters would win top billing in a women's liberation rogues' gallery. To say they are politically incorrect would not begin to describe the reality. Theirs is primarily a man's world, lived in the out-of-doors. Poor Ma would have a hard time explaining to Jake the inadequacies of her living arrangements. For Jake and his kind, a house is principally just a place to eat and sleep. They live out where the work is.

Some have said that Ace's pre–World War II generation was the last real "horseback" generation in the ranching industry. It has been claimed with some justification that the industry changed less from the 1880s to the beginning of World War II than in the first ten or fifteen years after the war. Into the early 1940s, cowboys still spent far more time on horseback than they spent in pickups and trucks.

My own memory goes back to the tail end of the 1920s. When my father went to work for the McElroy Ranch Company at Crane, Texas, in 1929, the ranch still used a chuckwagon drawn by a team of horses or mules, and most travel across the ranch was done on horseback or in a wagon. Within a couple of years after becoming foreman, Dad decided the chuckwagon was slow and inflexible, and he began mounting the chuckbox on the back of a truck.

The cow work remained the same, however. The crew, including short-term day-working hands, stayed out with the "wagon" twice a year, a week or so in the late summer and three to four weeks in the fall, branding, weaning, gathering calves and yearlings for sale or movement to winter pasturage. Except for the truck replacing the wagon, the work was still done much as my grandfather would have done it in the 1890s and early 1900s.

Though the ranch had been fenced into pastures, many were large enough that it took fully two days to work them. The wagon cook moved camp as needed, sometimes after one day, sometimes after two or three. During the "works" the hands took their meals from outdoor Dutch ovens and slept on the ground as their fathers and grandfathers had done.

Like most ranchers, Dad was always looking for a way to improve efficiency, though not necessarily our comfort. Often he would get us out of bed at four or five in the morning, and after a quick breakfast we would saddle up and ride for miles to reach the pasture where we were to do the day's work. When we were done, however early or late that might be, we rode home on horseback. Dad had observed some early homemade horse trailers and saw them as a potential time-saver. He experimented, taking an old truck chassis and building a plain open-topped wooden box on top of it, with a rear gate. Soon we were hauling our horses to the job, saving most of the time it took to ride there and back. This way we were able to work one pasture in the morning and another halfway across the ranch that afternoon—twice the work without using extra cowboys.

As Texas teacher-folklorist Paul Patterson has said, "Two things you never see anymore are a cowboy riding or a horse walking."

All across the West in the 1930s, other ranchers were upgrading their operations in similar ways. But once a cowboy was on horseback, he still handled cattle in basically the same ways as before.

As had been the case since the beginning of the range cattle industry, a majority of working cowboys were young bachelors. For the average hand, it would not become a lifelong trade. Most had to seek another way to make a living once they took on family responsibilities. The average ranch had few if any provisions for married cowboys except for foremen and perhaps line-camp men, who lived in isolation in areas distant from ranch headquarters, nor was the pay high enough to support a family in any style. Changes were still of a superficial nature.

This was the era in which Ace was growing up and first learning to make a hand. It was the time in which he was storing up the knowledge and experience that he would draw upon when he began his career as a cowboy cartoonist.

The war would bring changes few would have anticipated. A shortage of labor made it imperative for ranchers to use as many labor-saving, time-saving methods as they could. The age of the young bachelor cowboys, drifting from job to job as the spirit moved them, was basically over. Most of them went into military service and after the war chose not to return to the ranch, at least not on the same basis as before. To find labor, ranchers had to provide facilities for families and improve the pay scales. They changed many of their methods of work.

This was the new world Ace found when he went back to Electra after his wartime service. Like others who had grown up in the same period, he had one foot in the Old West and one in the new. And while the new offered many advantages, taking some of the rougher edges off of ranch life, there always remained some nostalgia for what had been left by the wayside.

ACE'S PRINCIPAL CHARACTER is a lanky cowboy named Jake, most often accompanied by his sidekick Zeb. Jake is highly flexible. Sometimes he is a small shirttail rancher with only a toenail hold, perennially skirting the edge of disaster. Other times he is a working cowboy in someone else's hire. No matter his situation, and allowing some exaggeration for effect, he reflects the realities of ranch life as Ace knew it in his formative years, mainly the 1930s and 1940s, and in his mature years, the 1950s and onward.

He always had a lot of fun at the expense of outsiders who did not understand the cowboy or the ranching business. A particular target was the deer hunters who annually flock into the Texas hill country to terrorize the whitetail deer herd. Living in Kerrville, he observed them firsthand. The hunters in Ace's cartoons are always ignorant of cowboy ways. In one a hunter has just killed a rancher's cow and declares that deer hunting is a snap. "Now, let's go get a turkey," he says. Ace often depicted hunters as being far more interested in drinking and playing poker in camp than in getting out and rousting the local deer.

Of course, we all know that Ace's cowboys would be just as lost on the streets of Houston as the Houston hunters are in the limestone hills of the Edwards Plateau. And it is an economic fact of life, especially in the hill country, that the revenue from hunters is all that keeps some ranchers afloat. Many ranchers grit their teeth and dread the opening of deer season, yet know that hunting fees are the margin between profit and loss.

Ace often lampooned real-estate salesmen, who were everlastingly trying to present the best image for droughted-out, cactus-studded, rock-strewn ranches of the kind Ace knew so well. He also saved a barb now and then for politicians, who promised much but fell far short on delivery.

Seldom did he portray a minister in anything but the best light. One cartoon I always liked shows the minister greeting rancher Jake, who is wearing his best and perhaps only suit. The minister says, "It's good to see you back. What is it this time? A drought or a break in the cattle market?"

Having grown up around livestock traders, Ace often depicted "Honest Wilbur, the Hoss Trader," who could find beauty in anything he was trying to sell but never in anything he was trying to buy. Wilbur always reminded me of a horse

Wul, I didn't tell you that ol' hoss would pitch,
cause the feller I bought 'em from didn't tell me, so I thought it wuz a secret!

February 18, 1973

trader with whom my father used to deal on occasion. Once he tried to sell Dad a young horse that he swore would never buck. The cowboy who got on him was thrown high enough to have grabbed a passing hawk. Dad protested, "You said that horse wouldn't buck. How come you to lie to me?" The trader calmly replied, "That's the way I sell horses."

Ace Reid knew the type and delighted in drawing them. They were not exactly crooked, necessarily, but as an old-timer said of a man I used to know, "He's a nice feller, but he'll bear some watchin'." There are still some horse traders left out in the hinterlands, but their cultural heirs are used-car and real-estate salesmen . . . and politicians.

Economics is a perennial subject of Ace Reid cartoons, especially as it applies to ranching. Ace's characters seem always on the verge of bankruptcy, as in the cartoon where Jake has just nailed up a "for sale" sign and says he is forced to sell because of his health. "I'm sick of starvin'," he explains.

Prosperity is always a fleeting phenomenon, like rainy spells. As one cartoon points out, it is hard to enjoy the good times for dread of the inevitable day when they will end, just as it is difficult to get full pleasure from a good rain because of the knowledge that sooner or later it will stop.

Jake's tightly twisted banker is sometimes called Mr. Tuffernell and other times Mr. Tuffernal. Under either name, the banker knows the realities. They are evident in his steely-eyed stare as Jake relates his latest tale of hard times.

It should be noted, however, that often the banker is the rancher's best friend, and now and then this shows in an Ace Reid cartoon for those who read between the lines. Operating loans are the lifeblood of the livestock industry. The average rancher must depend at least partly upon borrowed money for running expenses until he sells his calf crop, his lambs, his wool or mohair. Only a minority have the resources to operate on their own funds exclusively. In effect, the banker holds the power of economic life or death.

During the depression, and later the agonizingly long drought of the 1950s, compassionate bankers were often the difference between a rancher's staying on the land and liquidating. Indeed, some bankers risked their own careers by continuing to extend credit to people they considered good operators, though every rule in the book said the ranchers were in deep water over their heads and had no chance to survive.

Sometimes banker Tuffernell has to save Jake from his own shaky judgment by saying no to one of Jake's well-meant but risky notions.

Ace's characters often have problems with not only the banker but the Internal Revenue Service. Jake is not much of a bookkeeper. Like most old-time ranchers, he has a simple formula. He looks at his bank account at the first of each year. If it is larger than the year before, he has shown a profit. If it is smaller, he has shown a loss. Ace's kind of ranchers keep their records scrawled on a barn door or piled in a shoebox.

Like it or not, the IRS's demand for specifics has forced ranchers and farmers to become better bookkeepers than they used to be. I suspect Ace always preferred the old way. Sometimes ignorance can be bliss.

Jake's economic situation is summed up in a classic cartoon where a highway patrolman has stopped him because his pickup is sagging under a huge load of livestock feed. Jake complains, "I'm over-worked, over-drawn, over-taxed, and now I'm over-loaded!"

Weather is one of the most critical factors in a rancher's life, and Ace devoted many of his cartoons to that subject. Almost always the weather seems to be bad, usually because of droughty winds carrying a burden of dust or a winter snowstorm making life miserable for cattle, horses, and people. Only occasionally is the problem excessive rain, as in a cartoon which shows a cowboy commenting, "We had 14 inches of rain this year, all in one night." In another, Jake worries about being unable to get over a flooded road to his mailbox to pick up his drought-relief check.

As Ace's biographer John Erickson has written, the cowboy is defined by his work, and Ace always devoted much of his attention to the cowboy at his job. Often the subject matter is the confrontation with new ways of doing things . . . the intricacies of using a calf table instead of simply roping and throwing the calf down; the prospect of a huge stack of cedar posts and fencing wire that must be put to use; the fact that modern conveniences have done nothing to change a few of the basic truths of ranch life: the fighting nature of wild horses and wild cattle, the back-breaking reality of posthole diggers, or the indispensable nature of baling wire.

The magic of Ace Reid cartoons is that anyone familiar with country life, especially ranch life, can readily relate to them. Just about everyone knows a Jake, or perhaps a dozen of them, and many readers are Jake. Many a ranch woman can identify with long-suffering Ma, for there are few who have not gone through some of Ma's experiences. I can see some of my own mother in her, and particularly my grandmother, who for years used to cook for cowboys on the ranch where my grandfather was foreman. She was not paid extra for it; it was simply a duty expected of a foreman's wife in those times.

Many a rancher's wife has had to do without a piece of furniture she wanted or drive the old car a year or two longer because her husband saw a bull he did not think his cow herd could get along without.

Some aspects of ranch life have been changing rapidly since Ace's passing, and not always for the better. Margins have continued to erode. The cost of everything the rancher buys keeps ratcheting upward, while prices of the products he sells have lagged behind or even fallen. The result has been that many operators have been forced out of business through no fault of their own. Environmental pressures moreover have built to the point that sometimes government has more to say about what ranchers can do on their land than they do. Self-appointed, self-anointed "ecologists" are making many decisions for them, often to their economic detriment. Ace worried over that trend, and he would truly be troubled if he could see how far it has gone. It would have provided grist for many a cartoon, not all of them funny.

Ace was a rancher himself, in a limited way. When his cartoons began paying off, he bought a small ranch north of Kerrville and delighted in referring to it as the Dragging S. He built a house for Madge and a studio for himself. The studio straddled a beautiful running creek, so that Ace could look out his window and down into the gurgling water. Water is always at a premium in West Texas.

Much of Ace Jr.'s wit was inherited from his father. After Ace bought his ranch, Old Man Ace went down to see it. Ace left his father beside the creek when he was called to the telephone. Returning, as he liked to tell the story, he found Ace Sr. sitting on a rock with tears running down his cheeks. "Old Man Ace," he demanded, "what in the world is the matter with you?"

Ace Sr. replied, "Son, I've been a cowman all my life. I've hunted water, I've hauled water, I've pumped water for a bunch of thirsty old cows as long as I can remember. And to see all this runnin' to waste is more than I can stand."

Some fans who did not know there were both an Ace Sr. and an Ace Jr. would occasionally take one of Ace's cartoon books or calendars to the old man for his autograph. He would sign them without letting on. "After all," he said, "all Son done was draw the pictures. I was the one that lived the life."

Ace eventually came to be in such demand as a speaker that he found it getting in the way of his cartooning and other activities. He set his rates high enough that he thought he would scare off a lot of prospects, but evidently it did not discourage enough to hurt him. He made it a point to honor every commitment no matter how difficult. Once, due to speak to a group of Dakota cattle ranchers, he found that a blizzard had grounded the airplanes. He rented a car and drove through a snowstorm so severe he could hardly see the road, but he got there.

It is common to say that someone you meet reminds you of someone else. I never could say that Ace reminded me of anyone I knew, for he was unique. He was one of those singular people who stand completely alone in memory, the kind of whom you meet only a few during an average lifetime. He was fun-loving, sometimes to excess, liking nothing better than to pull a practical joke. Some he committed with his friend and partner in crime Hondo Crouch are legendary among people who knew the pair. Expansive and outgoing, he never let anyone around him remain a stranger for long. He was effusive with his praise and very spare with any criticism.

He was more sentimental than he liked to let the public know. The death of Hondo Crouch left him devastated. I'll never forget a telephone call I received from him the day he found out that another buddy, movie actor Slim Pickens, was dying. Ace could hardly speak. He held his friendships dear, and each loss hurt him deeply.

One way he showed his friendship was by making his friends the butts of jokes in his cartoons. He delighted in putting Charlie Schreiner III's YO brand on the poorest, boniest cow brutes he could draw. More than once, I found my name on a jailhouse wall in an Ace Reid cartoon, along with those of cowboy poet S. Omar Barker and bronc rider Casey Tibbs.

Ace passed under the shadow of death in the early 1960s, when he was diagnosed with leukemia, blamed on exposure to radiation from atomic bomb blasts in the Pacific while he was in the Navy. He beat the odds for thirty more years, finally dying November 10, 1991, after a period of declining health. He was sixty-six.

A conventional church service was conducted in Kerrville, followed by a cowboy funeral service at his ranch. His friend Cliff Teinert sang a cowboy benediction, and a riderless horse was led past the mourners, with Ace's boots backward in the stirrups. Ace's ashes were scattered over the ranch in accordance with his wishes. He had said, "Anywhere an old cow stops to graze a blade of grass, I'll be there."

There have been and still are other cowboy cartoonists, and each has found his own individual niche, but no one has ever duplicated the distinctive flavor of Ace's work any more than anyone has ever duplicated J. R. Williams, Charles M. Russell, or Frederic Remington. No one should ever try, for each was one of a kind.

WORK

Hey, Jake! It says here, "Cowboys have a glamorous and excitin' life."

October 9, 1955

Wal, now, ain't we the purty one!

November 25, 1956

Yep, I hauled my milk cow over this road once
and she didn't give nothin' but buttermilk for a week.

January 27, 1957

Yep, we finally got her loaded, but the question is now—
how long will what's left of the trailer last?

June 30, 1957

What I want to know is how are we gonna get down to that top soil?

September 7, 1958

Dang it! Fer 40 years I been hopin' to get through jist one roundup without this!

September 21, 1958

Watch out there, Jake! Don't skin up that ol' heifer!

January 11, 1959

Shore, I said bring everything out of the brush, but I only meant the cattle!

December 13, 1959

Well, how wuz I to know? The boss jist asked: "You want a job
where you can start from the top?"

February 7, 1960

One thing, for shure—if it weren't for that loose fence,
we'd been outa grass a long time ago.

August 6, 1961

Hey, Jake, how about your coffee break?

December 3, 1961

We gotta get longer-legged cattle or pastures that ain't so rough.

March 25, 1962

Says here that this soap makes yore undies white as snow
and keeps yore hands soft and lovely.

December 16, 1962

The boss said that we oughta be inspired by the fact we're developin'
the vast resources of the great West.

March 24, 1963

I'm shore learnin' the livestock business,
it took five years 'fore I went broke this time!

December 15, 1963

O−O−O−Oh what a beautiful mornin'!!

March 8, 1964

At least we're gittin' to work in the shade.

September 6, 1964

Better rope that ole steer now, cause the brush is liable to start gittin' thick!

July 25, 1965

Gosh, it's so hot my 5-day deodorant played out on them first three holes.

August 22, 1965

Yonder is a good shady place to have this flat in!

September 5, 1965

In home after dark and leave out before daylight . . . it shore don't take long
to spend the night on this place!

January 9, 1966

I ain't trying to ride him . . . I'm lookin' fer a clear spot to land!

April 23, 1967

Son, you'll never be a good cowboy unless you can tell
when one more piece of balin' wire will break a shed down!

May 14, 1967

Now brand 'em easy fer as thin as they are you might brand right through 'em.

May 28, 1967

Open yore eyes, Jake! You can't look for cattle with yore eyes closed.

July 23, 1967

The government is always helpin' us dig tanks and build fence,
I jist wonder if we could git 'em to help us gather these ole brushy steers.

January 28, 1968

If I live through this, I'm gonna apply fer one them civil service jobs.

February 11, 1968

Yea, and raisin' that beef will do the same thing too!

March 24, 1968

I've been ranching on this place fer 40 years and my best year I only lost $500!

June 2, 1968

The trouble with this big ole ranch is there ain't anyplace to ever take a short cut!

July 28, 1968

Hoss, times have shore changed. When I was a kid I had to ride the tough hosses
fer the old men . . . now I'm old and I hafta ride 'em fer the kids!

September 8, 1968

It usta be when I went to the brandin' pens all I needed wuz a good rope
and a hoss . . . now I need an oil can and a crescent wrench.

January 19, 1969

I wintered mighty good . . . all my cows are still standin' up!

May 12, 1974

Did the boss say dig them holes 2 feet apart and 10 feet deep
er 10 feet apart and 2 feet deep?

February 12, 1989

ECONOMICS

Man, this is better'n bein' rich.
Jist owe everybody so much they gotta be nice to you.

December 16, 1956

Wal, I jist can't enjoy any of this prosperity fer dreadin' the day
when the bottom falls out agin!

July 12, 1959

Can't see what them income tax boys are so mad about.
I got all my figures wrote down, ain't I?

December 17, 1961

Wul heck! I'm over-worked, over-drawn, over-taxed
and now I'm over-loaded!

February 18, 1962

No, you can't deduct a banker and three feed salesmen as your dependents!

April 12, 1964

Income . . . what's that?

April 18, 1965

There's something wrong when a feller spends his whole life raisin' leather
and still can't afford to wear it.

March 30, 1969

Zeb, sumpin' has to be done about this inflation,
the cost of livin' is up $1.00 a case!

May 18, 1975

Hot Dog—we got our check fer our wool,
now we can afford to go to the Cattlemen's Convention.

November 23, 1975

Whattaya mean, pay my bills?
If I had any money, I wouldn't have charged 'em in the first place!

February 15, 1976

Awright, I want $500.00 fur this hoss and you offer me $50.00,
wul I ain't gonna let $450.00 stand in the way of a sale.

August 27, 1978

Now that's what's keeping me broke—the easy monthly payments!

September 2, 1979

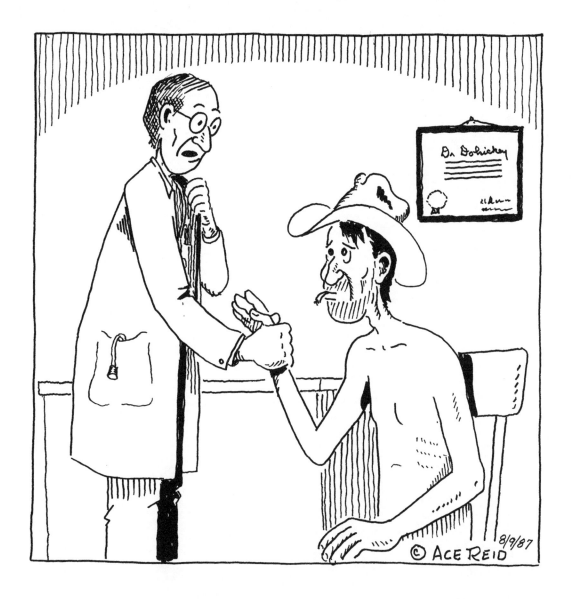

I've got good news, Jake, you got arthritis, you can't afford bursitis!

August 9, 1987

BANKERS

Come on, I jist found out we got more grass than credit.

March 16, 1958

Certainly 20% interest is too much, but it ain't near enough when
you're loanin' money to a bunch of crazy cow traders!

February 21, 1960

No. That ain't his preacher prayin'. That's his banker!

August 27, 1961

I bet you won't believe them cows I had mortgaged got struck by lightnin'
and all them unmortgaged ones had twin calves.

April 29, 1962

Jist make that note for EVER, but I'll shore try to git it paid off 'fore thet!

June 17, 1962

Look, one's tryin' to hide 'cause he's scared the Banker wants his money back and the other one's scared 'cause he's afraid Jake's gonna want to borrow more.

November 25, 1962

No, he didn't let me have no money, but he shore gave me lots of advice.

October 11, 1964

Yes sir, I been lyin' to you all along . . . ain't that expected of a good cowtrader?

March 7, 1965

Sir, ain't much wrong with the livestock business, 'cept cheap cattle, big feed bills, early winter, late spring and a dry summer at 12% interest!

June 20, 1965

Naw, I ain't got the flu, I'm sufferin' from a banker's chilly reception.

January 2, 1966

Sure, Jake, I could loan you that much money, but you'd just spend it!

March 13, 1966

. . . and I'll pay you off jist as soon as we git a long wet spell
and a high cow market!

April 2, 1967

Mr. Tufernal, you said you wanted yer money er my cows . . . wul, here's my cows!

August 13, 1967

Naw, Jake, I can't cash your check, it ain't that you're overdrawn,
it's yere jist under deposited!

April 25, 1971

Awright "Tuffy," if you ain't gonna loan me any money,
I jist might go to Arabia and borrow it!

August 17, 1975

Banker Tufernal said I wuzn't only under capitalized but I wuz also over financed!

May 22, 1988

WEATHER

The thing about these droughts—it gives a fella time to forgit
jist how muddy a dang cowlot can git.

September 22, 1957

I hope this grasshopper situation improves soon. This one jist ate the milk cow.

July 27, 1958

One good thing about it, we shore won't have to chop the ice off this trough.

December 28, 1958

Golly, the temperature's droppin' so fast it's pullin' the thermometer off the wall!

January 14, 1962

Ain't no use agoin' to look at that pasture. Jist sit down and watch it go by.

March 18, 1962

Maw, ain't this rain wonderful . . . jist makes a feller wanta git right out in it!

June 11, 1967

Zeb, wouldn't it be awful livin' in one of them big towns with all that air pollution!

July 16, 1967

On this farm you don't even hafta rotate the crops,
the wind rotates the soil fer you!

February 25, 1968

We had 14 inches of rain this year, all in one night.

February 9, 1975

I'm plantin' a garden, gonna grow frozen vegetables!

March 9, 1975

We've got a flat!

April 13, 1975

Wul the radiator is froze, the heater's quit, and I guess we would freeze to death
if I hadn't put this cardboard in the window!

March 1, 1981

If this wind don't lay soon somebody oughta take that collar offa that dog!

May 24, 1987

Boy it's hot when you see a dog chasin' a rabbit and they're both walkin'!

August 2, 1987

MA

Come on, Ma. Who ever heard tell of it taking two hours jist to buy
a sack of chicken feed?

June 9, 1957

My gosh, Jake, during the drought you cried about not makin' any money.
Now you're cryin' 'cause you made some.

April 12, 1959

Miss, would you please gift wrap this? It's fer my wife's Christmas present.

December 20, 1959

Maw's hollerin' fer a fur coat, so wrap these up. She can catch her own!

December 24, 1961

Maw, if you can give up a few of your luxuries, we can buy that adjoinin' land.

March 4, 1962

Ma, I can't help you dig now, cause I'm busy a-thinkin'.

April 8, 1962

Of course, Ma, we could have nicer things if I'd jist inherited money
'stead of good looks!

May 27, 1962

So what if it is cold in the barn . . . at least it'll smell better!

January 5, 1964

The meat's fried too hard, the biscuits are soggy and the coffee's weak
. . . but . . . but, that's the way I like 'em!

March 28, 1965

No, Jake, I don't think the fashionable short skirts could make me look any sexier!

December 5, 1965

I want 3 sacks of that print in case me and Maw are invited to Luci Johnson's weddin' Maw will have a new dress.

February 27, 1966

Maw, you wanted to have a picnic under shade trees on the bank of a creek . . .
wal, here we are!

August 21, 1966

Doc, when you find out what's the matter with Domino,
maybe you'd look at Maw. She's got the same symptoms!

February 5, 1967

Paw, I shore hope that ole hen didn't have as much trouble layin' them eggs
as you did gatherin' 'em!

April 9, 1967

Maw, don't be so dumb about openin' a gate . . . jist take it off the hinges!

March 3, 1968

Maw, you think you're hot . . . you oughta be under this old tin roof like me!

April 21, 1968

Jake, you're gonna hafta git this pickup worked on . . . the reverse won't work!

September 29, 1968

No, it's nothin' serious, I jist went dancin' with Jake Saturday night!

November 3, 1968

Wul, we're stuck, Ma! You run to the house and get help and I'll stay here
and keep the motor runnin' so the radiator won't freeze!

January 12, 1969

Maw, you pay the bill, I'll go lock these groceries up in the glove compartment so they'll be safe.

January 5, 1975

Wul, Maw, countin' the fertilizer, labor, water and the seeds—
we don't have over $14.65 in this tomater!

June 8, 1975

Jake, we're havin' a seafood dinner tonight. Sardines and navy beans.

July 20, 1975

Jake, I can't tell how much it's rained—the gauge is running over!

February 29, 1976

Maw, I love you because you're gorgeous, sexy, and a heck of a gate opener!

May 30, 1976

Maw, did you remember to bring in the wood?

May 22, 1977

We're makin' a survey of how many energy conserving devices
are being used in your home.

January 14, 1979

Maw, yore'd better leave them spiders alone. Yore might upset
the balance of nature.

March 11, 1979

Maw, I want to make a deal with you, I'll stop nippin' if you stop naggin'!

October 12, 1986

Gosh, I wish Maw would come home. I'm tired of washin' my own clothes!

August 30, 1987

Oh, I tried countin' sheep, I got to 5000, sheared 'em, shipped 'em,
and still lost money!

September 11, 1988

[140]

OUTSIDERS

© ACE REID

Hey, could you fellows tell us where we might see real cowboys?

August 7, 1955

I was sent here to collect $5, but if you will jist show me how to get out of here,
I'll give you $5.

April 1, 1956

Perfect, Mister! Our readers sure like action pictures.

September 23, 1956

You might think you're a cowboy, but them critters ain't figured it out yet!

April 25, 1959

Yep, folks, if you don't mind droughts, dust, tornadoes, snakes, spiders and stingin' scorpions, you're gonna love this place!

May 24, 1959

Boys, shore looks like we forgot one thing . . . the guns.

November 17, 1963

Sir, would you please tell us why you carve initials on those cows?

July 12, 1964

No, it ain't always terrible hot here, sometimes it's miserable windy
or unbearable cold!

August 9, 1964

Jake, on second thought, let's jist eat 'em here!

November 15, 1964

If you desire a place that's quiet and has a dry climate,
there's about two million acres here you'll love!

May 21, 1967

Now this ranch will run a cow to the section . . . if you feed a lot!

June 4, 1967

Wul, boys, I guess you have all yore huntin' necessities . . . five cases of whiskey and a box of shells!

November 12, 1967

Mr. Newcomer, you say you want to buy my cow and learn the business.
Well, this cow has bangs, lump jaw and a spoiled udder
and I guarantee you'll learn from her.

December 17, 1967

Did anybody think to bring a gun, in case a deer gets in here?

December 7, 1975

Now this is what you call "Owning a piece of the rock!"

July 20, 1980

Naw, they ain't revolutionist . . . jist deer hunters goin' to camp!

November 24, 1985

FRIENDS & NEIGHBORS

And with the roar of a .45, Cactus clutched his bloody chest
and fell face down in the dirt.

January 12, 1958

This place shore outta be a National Park . . . ain't no trees or mountains
or nothin' clutterin' up the scenery.

September 23, 1962

Now from here on, this part of the county voted Republican!

February 7, 1965

Naw, we ain't upset about world affairs, somebody stole our double six!

April 25, 1965

Yeah, she and I was hittin' it off fine, drinking beer and holding hands,
then I find out he's a car salesman from California!

October 4, 1970

I jist gotta new diet, my doctor put me on fried steak, gravy, mashed potatoes
and pie—said he wanted me to die happy!

June 23, 1974

Jake, I came out here to talk to you about the church,
but after havin' to open and close all your gates, I've lost my religion too!

July 13, 1975

Well, he's got a right to howl. Them environmentalist fellers
have protected him 'til there ain't a sheep left in the country!

August 31, 1975

Yessir, if I'd known I was gonna live this long, I'd've taken better care of myself!

February 22, 1976

It's good to see you back. What is it this time? A drought
or a break in the cattle market?

June 24, 1969

Yore gonna go free. No where in this law book does it say it's illegal
to steal a sorrel hoss with four stockin' legs.

July 31, 1988

I had to quit drinkin', why by nine o'clock I was so smart
I couldn't find anybody intelligent enough to talk to.

August 7, 1988

Hey, Jake, throw that cigarette away, the Surgeon General says
they're harmful to your health!

September 4, 1988

Jake, I'm yore County Commissioner and I wuz drivin' up here to ask you
to vote fer me, but yore road is so bad I got stuck!

October 23, 1988

Wul the coyotes and mountain lions have eaten about all our calves and sheep.
I'm shore gettn' tired of livin' on fresh air and scenery!

December 11, 1988

DESIGN AND TYPOGRAPHY BY GEORGE LENOX

Printed and bound by CPI Group (UK) Ltd, Croydon, CR0 4YY

13/04/2025

14656495-0002